Mind Mechanics

Delving Deep into the Gears of Cognitive Psychology

Freudian Trips

Copyright Page

Disclaimer

The views and opinions expressed in this book are those of the author(s) and do not necessarily reflect the official policy or position of any other agency, organization, employer, or company. The contents of this book are for informational and educational purposes only and are not intended to serve as professional advice, diagnosis, or treatment.

The information provided in this book is believed to be accurate and reliable as of the date of publication. However, it may include some errors or inaccuracies, and no warranty or guarantee is provided regarding the accuracy, timeliness, or applicability of the content.

Readers are encouraged to consult with professional philosophers, educators, or other qualified professionals where appropriate for personalized advice. The author(s) and publisher shall not be liable for any loss, damage, or harm caused or alleged to be caused, directly or indirectly, by the information or ideas contained, suggested, or referenced in this book.

By reading this book, the reader acknowledges and agrees that they are solely responsible for how they interpret and apply the information contained herein.

This book may also include references to other works, studies, and sources. These references are provided for further reading and exploration and do not imply endorsement or validation of the specific theories, viewpoints, or interpretations presented in those works.

Chapter 1: Embarking on a Mind Journey

If you've ever had the thrill of standing at the foot of a mountain, staring at its looming peaks and thinking, "What would it be like at the top?", then you know the exhilaration of being at the beginning of a journey. That's exactly where you are now, at the base of a metaphorical mountain. Instead of climbing steep crags, however, you're about to traverse the intricate and fascinating landscape of the human mind.

Why Are We Here?

Imagine trying to unravel the mysteries of a machine without a manual. The human brain, with its billions of neurons and countless connections, often feels like such a machine. Yet, it's not just any machine. It's the masterpiece of nature that allows us to think, feel, dream, and create. Wouldn't it be wondrous to have a guide that simplifies and deciphers its workings?

That's what this book sets out to do.

Our Expedition Map

So, what can you expect from this book? Here's a brief rundown:

Exploring the Mind's Landscapes: From the way we remember a childhood memory to the reason we might prefer coffee over tea, the book offers insights into the daily wonders of our cognition.

The Mind's Bridges and Barriers: Ever wondered why sometimes ideas just 'click', while other times they feel like distant fog? We'll unravel these intricacies.

Interactions and Connections: The dance between emotion, thought, and action. Why do we feel the way we feel, and how does it guide our actions?

Future Gazing: How is the digital world changing the way our brains work? And what new frontiers are scientists exploring now?

But this isn't just a simple map. No, it's a dynamic journey! Along the way, there will be stories, examples, and little experiments that you can try yourself. Imagine not just reading about the mind, but actively engaging with it!

Why This Expedition Matters

To many, understanding the mind might seem like a lofty goal, reserved only for scientists and researchers. But think about it: every decision we make, every dream we chase, and every interaction we have is shaped by the intricate workings of our minds.

By embarking on this journey, you're not just gaining knowledge;

you're gaining insight into yourself, the people around you, and the world at large. It's a ticket to better decisions, deeper understanding, and a richer life experience.

Your Role in This Journey

You're not just a passive traveler here. You're an explorer. Ask questions, draw parallels with your own experiences, and reflect on what you discover. There will be moments of wonder, moments of introspection, and countless "Aha!" moments.

So, whether you're here out of pure curiosity, a thirst for knowledge, or maybe even just stumbled upon this journey by chance, welcome. By the end, the hope is that you'll not only understand the wonders of the human mind a little better but also marvel at your own cognitive capabilities.

Are you ready, fellow voyager? Let's begin this mind journey.

Chapter 2: Opening the Door to Our Inner World

Remember those intriguing treasure chests in old tales and movies, filled with secrets and wonders? Our minds are just like those chests. In this chapter, we will peek inside that box and glimpse its treasures, and we will also meet some of the key locksmiths who've helped us understand how to unlock its mysteries.

The Treasure Chest Called 'Cognitive Psychology'

Alright, let's simplify this. If our brain was a computer, cognitive psychology would be like understanding the software – the programs and applications that make it run. It's about how we think, how we learn, how we remember things, why we forget, how we solve problems, and so much more.

Imagine being at a magic show. The magician performs tricks, and you're left baffled and amazed. Cognitive psychology is like being taken backstage to see how the tricks work. Instead of magic tricks, though, it's the everyday wonders of how our minds function.

Meet the Locksmiths: Pioneers of the Mind

While the story of understanding our mind has countless contributors, let's introduce a few rockstars of this world:

Jean Piaget: Picture a curious man watching children play, think, and interact. That's Piaget for you. He gave us deep insights into how children think differently than adults and how their minds develop.

Elizabeth Loftus: Have you ever been utterly sure you remembered something, only to discover you were wrong? Loftus explored the maze of our memory, revealing its flexibility and fallibility.

Noam Chomsky: If our thoughts were music, language would be its notes. Chomsky delved into how we understand and produce language, suggesting our brains have a built-in "blueprint" for it.

Daniel Kahneman: Ever made a silly mistake or a decision that now seems, well, irrational? Kahneman walked us through the short-cuts our brains often take, for better or worse.

These figures (and many more) lit the path into the mind's depths. Their discoveries, stories, and insights form the bedrock of what we'll explore.

Why This Journey Matters

You might wonder, "Why should I care about these scientists and their discoveries?" Well, imagine understanding:

Why you make certain decisions.

How your childhood experiences shape your adult thoughts.

Why certain songs or scents trigger powerful memories.

Understanding our cognitive processes isn't just academic; it's deeply personal and profoundly empowering. It's like gaining a user manual for your mind.

We stand at the door of a grand mansion - the human mind. With each chapter, each page, we'll explore its rooms, corridors, and secret chambers. As we do, remember those locksmiths, the pioneering figures who handed us the keys. With gratitude, curiosity, and wonder, let's step inside.

Onward to the adventure!

Chapter 3: Brainwork – Painting the Canvas of Thought

Imagine standing in front of a vast, white canvas, with a brush in hand and a palette full of vibrant colors. Each brushstroke represents a thought, an emotion, a memory. This is what our brain does – it paints the intricate masterpiece of our experiences. Welcome to the studio of cognitive psychology, where we'll delve into how this artistry comes alive!

Cognitive Psychology: The Art School of the Mind

In the simplest of terms, cognitive psychology is the study of how we think. But, isn't that too broad? Well, let's break it down.

Picture the mind as an art studio:

The Palette: This represents our memory, filled with a myriad of experiences, feelings, and knowledge. It's where we pick and choose colors (memories) to paint our present moment.

The Brushstrokes: These are our decisions. Every choice is a stroke on the canvas. Some are deliberate; others are more spontaneous.

The Canvas: Represents our attention. At any given moment, we can only paint on a certain part of it, focusing on specific things while leaving others in the periphery.

The Finished Artwork: This symbolizes our behavior and actions – the tangible results of all our thinking and feeling.

Exploring the Artistry: Cognitive Processes

Now, let's delve deeper into how we create our mind's artwork:

Sketching (Perception): Before we paint, we sketch. This is like perception - it's how we interpret the world around us using our senses. It's our initial outline of a situation, based on what we see, hear, touch, taste, and smell.

Choosing Colors (Memory): Our past experiences influence our present. Memory provides the colors, the past experiences and knowledge, that will be used to fill in our sketches.

Designing Patterns (Thinking): Here's where we plan and organize. It's about solving problems, making decisions, and forming judgments.

Layering (Emotion): Emotions add depth to our artwork. They provide the layers and texture, influencing the vibrancy or subtlety of our reactions.

Framing (Attention): Finally, we decide which part of our canvas to display prominently. Our attention shifts, deciding which parts of our artwork (or which thoughts and perceptions) get the limelight.

Understanding the processes of cognitive psychology is like gaining the tools and techniques to become a master artist of our own experiences. While we might not always control the events of our lives, understanding how we perceive, remember, think, and feel gives us the power to paint our reactions with intent and clarity.

So, dear reader, the next time you find yourself making a decision, recalling a memory, or simply daydreaming, remember—you're creating art. Appreciate the masterpiece that is your mind.

On to the next room of our grand mansion!

Chapter 4: Mind Maps – Crafting Our Inner Blueprints

Imagine walking into a city you've never visited before. The roads, the buildings, the parks – every bit of it has been planned and structured. Similarly, inside our minds, there's a blueprint for how we understand and interpret the world. Let's take a stroll through the cityscape of our thoughts!

Crafting Cities in the Mind

Before we delve deep, think about how a city is planned. There are residential zones, commercial areas, parks, and so on. Similarly, our mind organizes information into different 'zones' or structures, helping us navigate our experiences.

Conceptual Structures: Imagine these as the residential zones. These are categories or clusters where similar ideas live. For instance, under the category of "birds," we might think of sparrows, eagles, and penguins. They're all different, but they belong to the same neighborhood.

Mental Structures: These are the roads and pathways connecting different zones. For instance, when you think of a beach, it might lead you to thoughts about the sea, which in turn might remind you of a cruise, and so on. These connections are the mental pathways that help thoughts flow.

Building Blocks: Schema and Scripts

Now, imagine you're visiting a new building in our thought city. How do you know where the entrance is, or how to navigate its rooms? That's where our mind's building blocks, schema and scripts, come into play.

Schema (Blueprints): Think of schemas as the general blueprints for buildings. They're our brain's way of organizing information. For instance, when you think of a "school," a schema forms in your mind with classrooms, teachers, students, and books. It's the general idea or structure we have about something, based on our experiences.

Scripts (Guided Tours): These are the standard sequences of events in specific situations. For instance, there is a standard procedure when you visit a restaurant: you are seated, read the menu, place your order, eat, and then pay. Similar to a tour guide leading us through a building, scripts assist us anticipate and comprehend what will happen next.

Our minds aren't just a jumble of random thoughts and memories. They are meticulously organized, much like a well-planned city. Every thought, experience, or piece of knowledge has its own place, its own address in our mental cityscape.

Understanding this architecture empowers us. It means we can better comprehend why certain memories surface, why some thoughts lead to others, and how our experiences shape the cities within our minds.

So, the next time you find yourself lost in thought, remember—you're simply strolling through the beautiful streets of your inner city. Enjoy the journey, and don't forget to marvel at its intricate planning!

Onward, as we continue to explore the grandeur of our minds!

Chapter 5: The Conscious Conductor – Directing the Symphony of Sensation

Imagine being at a grand orchestra. There's a massive ensemble of instruments – violins, trumpets, flutes, drums – all playing their parts. Yet, amidst this cacophony, a conductor stands tall, guiding the musicians, emphasizing certain instruments while toning down others. This, dear reader, is a lot like how our attention and perception work. Ready to direct your own symphony?

The Maestro: Understanding Attention

In the grand concert of life, countless stimuli vie for our notice: sights, sounds, smells, and so on. But we can't possibly process everything at once! That's where attention steps in. It acts like our mind's conductor.

Selective Spotlight: Attention is like shining a spotlight on certain parts of the orchestra while dimming others. If you've ever been in a crowded room and suddenly heard someone mention your name, you know this feeling! Amongst all the chatter, your attention "spotlighted" something relevant to you.

Shifting Focus: Just as a conductor might move from emphasizing the strings to the brass, our attention can shift quickly between different stimuli. Ever found yourself watching a movie, only to get distracted by a sudden noise outside? That's your attention shifting!

The Orchestra: Grasping Perception

Now, while attention decides which part of the orchestra to emphasize, perception is all about interpreting the music that's being played.

Interpreting Notes (Perceiving Details): This is about understanding individual stimuli. For instance, seeing the color of a friend's dress or hearing the words of a song.

Crafting the Melody (Interpreting the Whole): Perception isn't just about individual details. It's also about understanding the bigger picture. When you recognize a familiar tune or grasp the theme of a story, that's your perception crafting a comprehensive melody from individual notes.

Theories: Understanding the Music Score

While our concert analogy provides a simple understanding, scientists and thinkers have proposed various models to explain these processes:

Filter Theory: Picture a stage with a curtain. Only the most important or loud instruments (stimuli) are allowed through the curtain into our awareness. Everything else remains muffled or unnoticed.

Resource Model: Imagine our attention as a limited set of resources. Just as an orchestra has a budget which decides which instruments can be included, our attention only has so much "currency" to spread across different stimuli.

These models, and others, are like music scores – they provide structured explanations for the otherwise complex concert of attention and perception.

Life is a grand, ongoing concert. Every moment, melodies of experiences play out around us. With our attention and perception, we not only select which parts of the orchestra to focus on but also interpret the music they produce.

So, the next time you're lost in thought or captivated by a sensation, remember: you're both the conductor and the audience in the beautiful symphony of life.

On to the next chapter, where we'll uncover more wonders of the mind!

Chapter 6: Memento - The Time Capsules of Our Mind

Think about your favorite childhood summer day, the lyrics of a catchy tune, or even the pattern you tie your shoelaces in. How do we keep track of all these? In the vast library of our mind, memories are the books that line the shelves. Let's step into this library and explore the stories within.

The Shelves: Different Types of Memories

Snapshots (Sensory Memory): Imagine taking quick photographs of everything you experience. Sensory memory holds onto these 'snapshots' for just a few seconds. It's that brief echo of a sound just after it ends or the flash of an image you just saw.

The Favorites Section (Short-term Memory): Think of this as the "Currently Reading" shelf. It's the place for memories we're currently using or thinking about, like recalling someone's phone number.

The Archive (Long-term Memory): These are the old classics, the volumes that tell the stories of our lives. From your first day at school to the skills you've acquired, like riding a bike – these memories can last a lifetime.

The Librarian: Memory Processes

Our library isn't just a static place. There's a lot going on!

Acquisition (Encoding): This is how new books (memories) get into our library. Every experience is translated into a format that our brain can store.

Organization (Storage): Once we've acquired a memory, it needs to be stored on the right shelf. The brain tucks it away for safekeeping.

Retrieval: When you want to recall a past holiday or the name of a friend, you're pulling a book off a shelf. This is how we access and bring memories to the forefront of our mind.

Decoding Memory: Theories and Ideas

While our library analogy simplifies things, the study of memory is vast. Here are some simplified theories:

The Notebook Theory (Atkinson-Shiffrin Model): This model describes memory as a progression. Information starts in sensory memory (a quick note), moves to short-term (a page in a notebook), and can then be saved into long-term memory (a finalized book).

The Web of Thoughts (Semantic Network Model): Imagine a vast spider web. Each thread connects different ideas. The closer two ideas are on the web, the more related they are. So thinking of "beach" might quickly lead you to think of "sand."

Our memory isn't just a repository but a living, breathing entity – always changing, updating, and reshuffling. It gives us continuity, identity, and a connection to our past, guiding our present and shaping our future.

So, every time you recall a fond memory or grasp a new piece of information, take a moment to marvel at the incredible library that rests within your mind.

Let's bookmark this chapter and prepare to journey even deeper in the next!

Chapter 7: Speak Your Mind – The Dance of Words and Wonders

Have you ever stopped to think about how marvelous it is that we can communicate complex emotions, vivid imaginations, or intricate plans just by stringing together sounds and symbols? The tango of language and thought is one of the most fascinating dances of the human mind. Let's discover the rhythm behind it.

Two Sides of a Coin: Language and Thought

Imagine watching a silent movie. Even without words, you grasp the story through gestures, expressions, and actions. But when dialogue is introduced, the narrative takes on deeper layers of meaning.

Language: It's the dialogue in our silent movie, the words and structures we use to express ourselves. Every sentence, every word choice, paints a richer picture.

Thought: These are the underlying stories, emotions, and concepts. They're the plot twists, the dramatic pauses, and the climactic scenes in our mental movies.

While we can have thoughts without language (like when you feel hungry or see a beautiful sunset), language enriches, refines, and communicates those thoughts to others.

Journey of a Word: Models of Language Processing

So, how does a thought turn into spoken or written words? Let's trace this journey:

The Birthplace of Words (Conceptualization): It all starts with an idea or emotion. You see a beautiful bird and want to comment on it.

Crafting Sentences (Formulation): Your mind then crafts a suitable sentence. This involves selecting words and arranging them in the right order. "Look at that beautiful blue bird!"

Voicing Out (Articulation): Finally, the muscles in your mouth, tongue, and throat work together to pronounce the words, making your thought audible to the world.

Growing Up with Language: Theories of Development

Just like learning to walk or sing, acquiring language is a journey. But how do we move from babbling babies to eloquent adults?

The Imitation Game: Some believe we're master copycats. We learn language by mimicking the sounds and sentences we hear around us.

Born to Speak (Nativist Theory): This idea suggests we're born with a natural knack for language. Just as birds instinctively know how to build nests, humans have an inbuilt ability to learn languages.

Social Interaction: Language isn't just about words; it's about communication. Some theories propose that our interactions with caregivers and our environment shape our language skills.

Language is the bridge between our inner worlds and the vast universe outside. It allows us to share dreams, debate ideas, console others, and celebrate joys. In the symphony of cognition, language is both the lyrics and the melody.

Next time you read a book, share a story, or simply chat with a friend, take a moment to appreciate the wondrous dance of language and thought that unfolds.

Stay tuned as we explore even more mysteries of the mind in the next chapter!

Chapter 8: Decision's Crossroads – Navigating the Labyrinths of the Mind

Imagine standing at a crossroads in a vast, winding maze. Some paths are straight and clear, while others are twisted and obscured. Every day, we face countless such mazes in our minds, whether deciding on lunch, choosing a career path, or even figuring out how to fix a broken gadget. Let's embark on this journey to understand how we navigate these crossroads.

Paths and Choices: Problem Solving & Decision Making

Problem Solving: This is the compass that helps you determine the direction you should take. It involves understanding the maze (the problem) and then figuring out the best route (the solution). Whether it's solving a puzzle or addressing a personal challenge, it's all about finding your way.

Decision Making: Now that you've mapped out possible routes, which one will you choose? This process involves evaluating options and then picking the one that seems the best fit. It's the act of committing to a particular path.

Roadblocks and Shortcuts: Bias, Heuristics, and Fallacies

As you navigate, you'll notice some intriguing aspects of the maze:

Bias: Imagine some paths in the maze are lit up, making them seem more appealing, while others are in shadow. These are our biases – unconscious influences that affect our choices. For instance, maybe you tend to choose the same lunch every day because it's familiar (a comfort bias).

Heuristics: These are shortcuts we take. Think of them as signposts in our maze that say things like, "This way is usually faster," or "Most people choose this path." They simplify complex problems. For example, if you've heard good things about a restaurant, you might decide to eat there without looking into other options (the "word of mouth" heuristic).

Fallacies: Sometimes, the signposts in our maze can mislead us. These are fallacies – mistaken beliefs or flawed logic patterns. For instance, thinking that just because it rained today and you wore your red coat, wearing the coat must cause rain (a false causality fallacy).

Every day, our minds are bustling with the activities of navigating, deciding, and solving. While it might seem daunting, remember: it's okay to take detours, learn from dead ends, and occasionally rely on shortcuts. After all, every explorer grows not just by reaching the destination but also by understanding the journey.

The next time you find yourself at a crossroads, take a moment to appreciate the intricate processes helping you choose your path. And as always, be prepared to embark on new adventures in the upcoming chapters!

Chapter 9: Seeing Through the Mind's Eye – The Grand Cinema of Consciousness

Picture this: a sprawling valley with rolling green hills, fluffy clouds passing by, and a vibrant rainbow stretching across the sky. Even if you're inside a room right now, your mind can paint this vivid scene effortlessly. Welcome to the realm of visual cognition – our mind's in-built movie theater. Let's take a seat and watch the show!

The Grand Screen: Cognition's Role in Visual Interpretation

Our eyes are like cameras, capturing scenes from the world. But it's our brain that turns these snapshots into a coherent movie, complete with emotions, interpretations, and understandings.

Setting the Scene: Before we even 'see' anything, our brains are primed with expectations. If you're in a forest, you're more likely to spot a camouflaged bird than if you were in a city, simply because you expect to see it there.

The Main Cast: We pay special attention to certain elements that stand out or are familiar to us. It's like focusing on the main characters in a movie while the extras blur in the background.

Plot Twists: Sometimes, our brain fills in gaps or corrects visual information. Ever mistake a mannequin for a person, or see a shape in the clouds? That's your mind adding its own plot twists!

Behind the Scenes: Models of Visual Cognition

While it may seem like a spontaneous production, our visual experiences are directed by some underlying scripts:

The Template Model: Imagine having a mental library of shapes and patterns. Whenever you see something, you match it with a template from this library. For example, recognizing a cat because it fits your mental template of what a cat looks like.

The Feature Analysis Model: Instead of whole templates, consider breaking down visuals into features – lines, curves, colors. Seeing a round shape with two dots and a curve might be interpreted as a smiling face. It's like recognizing an actor by their signature hairstyle or voice.

Our minds don't just see; they interpret, predict, and even imagine. Every glance is a story, every gaze a painting. The world we perceive isn't just made of light and shadows, but of memories, feelings, and expectations.

Next time you're watching a sunset, appreciating a piece of art, or even daydreaming, remember that you're not just using your eyes but the grand cinema of your consciousness. There's always more to 'see', so keep those mental projectors running!

Stay tuned as we journey deeper into the wonders of cognition in our upcoming chapters!

Chapter 10: The Emotional Tide – Riding the Waves of the Heart and Mind

Have you ever felt the butterflies in your stomach before a big event? Or the comforting warmth of a memory from childhood? Emotions aren't just feelings; they're the vibrant colors that paint our experiences. Dive in with us as we explore the captivating dance between our feelings and thoughts, where emotions don't just add depth to our cognition but actively shape it.

The Heart-Mind Ballet: Emotion & Cognition Interplay

Two Guides on a Journey: If cognition is our map, then emotions are our compass. While our thoughts help us chart the path, our emotions provide a sense of direction. Ever felt inexplicably drawn to a decision? That's your emotional compass at work.

Emotion's Mark on Memory: Emotions are like bookmarks. Moments colored by strong emotions – whether a joyful birthday or a nerve-wracking exam – tend to be etched deeper in our memory. They become stories we revisit time and again.

Mood-tinted Glasses: Our current emotions can color our perceptions. If you're feeling blue, a rainy day might seem melancholic. But if you're in love, it might feel incredibly romantic.

Behind the Feelings: Theories of Emotion in Cognitive Psychology

Understanding emotions is like understanding music – there's rhythm, melody, and dynamics. Here are some simplified ideas on how they play out:

The Feedback Loop: Think of it as a dance. You see a snake (the stimulus), your heart races (physiological response), and then you realize you're scared (emotion). Your emotional response is influenced by your bodily reaction.

Two-Step Tango: First, you have an immediate, raw emotional reaction to something (like a sudden jolt of fear). Then, you process and interpret it (realizing it's just a toy snake, not a real one). The emotion gets fine-tuned through cognition.

The Orchestra Model: Emotions aren't isolated notes; they're a combination. Happiness might be a blend of safety, excitement, and contentment. Our cognition helps us differentiate and mix these emotional 'notes' to create the symphony of our feelings.

Emotions and thoughts are inseparable companions, dancing gracefully through our lives. They challenge, support, and enrich each other in a continuous ebb and flow. To understand one without the other would be like hearing a song with either only lyrics or just the tune.

As you move forward, remember that embracing both your heart and mind is the key to navigating the multifaceted journey of life. And keep those dancing shoes on, because our exploration of the vast world of cognition is far from over!

Chapter 11: The Quantum Leap – Bridging the Gap Between Brainwaves and Thoughtwaves

Ever wondered about the universe inside your head? Just as the cosmos is filled with stars and galaxies, our brains brim with neurons and connections. It's the grand meeting ground of biology and thought, where electrical signals become ideas, and where chemistry becomes emotion. Fasten your seatbelts as we embark on a journey between the synapses and the psyche.

The Meeting of Two Worlds: When Cognitive Psychology Meets Neuroscience

The Magnificent Machine: At the core, our brain is an intricate network of cells, each firing and communicating. But when these cells work together, magic happens – thoughts form, memories linger, and decisions take shape. It's like billions of tiny stars coming together to form constellations in the night sky.

More Than Just Electric Buzz: The electric signals in our brain aren't just random noise. They are orchestrated tunes that give rise to our cognition. Imagine a grand piano – each key represents a neuron. When played in harmony, a beautiful melody (or thought) emerges.

Neuroscientific Revelations: The Insights that Shaped Cognitive Psychology

The Plastic Symphony: One of the most captivating discoveries is brain plasticity. Our brain isn't a rigid structure. Like clay, it reshapes and reforms based on experiences. Learning a new skill or adapting to a change? That's your brain composing a new tune.

Emotional Centers: Ever felt a rush of happiness or a pang of sadness? Specific areas in our brain light up with activity during these emotions. It's like having different musical sections in an orchestra, with each playing a role in our emotional concert.

Memory's Storage Room: While our memories feel intangible, they reside in tangible locations. The hippocampus, a tiny seahorse-shaped part, plays a pivotal role. Think of it as a librarian, cataloging and retrieving memories.

The melding of cognitive psychology and neuroscience is like understanding both the lyrics and the music of a song. It's where we bridge the tangible with the intangible, the physical with the abstract. As we delve deeper into this enthralling fusion, we uncover not just how we think, but the very essence of what makes us, us.

Stay curious, dear traveler, for the voyage of discovery never truly ends. The next chapters promise even more wonders, as we further unravel the enigma of our own minds!

Chapter 12: The Mind in the Digital Age – Navigating the Crossroads of Silicon and Synapses

Raise your hand if you've ever felt your phone vibrate, only to find no notifications waiting. Or if you've ever been engrossed in a virtual reality game, feeling every emotion as if you're truly 'inside' that world. Welcome to the intersection of the digital age and our mind, where pixels meet perceptions and where software entwines with the soul.

Pixelated Perceptions: How Tech Shapes Our Thought Patterns

The World in Our Pockets: With smartphones, we have a universe of information at our fingertips. While this offers immense knowledge, it can also lead to information overload, shaping how we think, filter, and even remember.

Virtual Realities, Real Emotions: VR games and experiences might be made of codes and graphics, but the emotions they elicit are as real as any. Fear, excitement, wonder – all proof of how tech can tap into our cognitive processes.

Instant Connectivity, Fleeting Focus: The constant buzz of notifications can scatter our attention. Instead of diving deep into one task, we often skim the surface of many. Our focus span has started mirroring our screen time: short, frequent bursts.

Designing with the Mind in Mind: Human-Computer Symbiosis

Intuitive Interactions: Ever noticed how some apps just 'feel' easy to use? That's cognitive psychology at play. By understanding how the mind works, designers create interfaces that flow with our natural thought processes.

Feedback Loops and Rewards: The 'ding' when you get a message, or the colorful animation when you level up in a game, are all tailored to give a sense of achievement and satisfaction. It's cognitive psychology's way of saying, "Well done!"

Personalized Experiences: Why does your music app seem to 'know' your mood? Or how does your fitness tracker motivate you just right? By understanding our cognitive habits, technology offers uniquely tailored experiences, almost like a digital extension of ourselves.

As the lines blur between the digital world and our own, understanding how we think and perceive becomes even more crucial. The symbiosis of cognitive psychology and technology isn't just about making cooler gadgets; it's about creating tools that enhance, empower, and resonate with the very essence of human experience.

Journey on, dear reader. As technology evolves, so does our understanding of ourselves. The future promises a blend of the human and the digital, and you're right at the heart of this thrilling merge!

Chapter 13: Echoes of the Future – Charting the Uncharted Terrains of the Mind

Have you ever looked up at the night sky, mesmerized by the stars, and wondered what lay beyond? That's the exact feeling when venturing into the mysteries of our mind. Cognitive psychology isn't a static field. Like the ever-expanding universe, our understanding of cognition constantly evolves. Join us as we soar into the vast unknowns, exploring the realms that are still being unveiled.

Beyond the Known: The New Frontiers of Cognitive Research

Brainwaves and Digital Realms: Today, scientists are merging the digital world with cognitive studies. Using virtual realities, they recreate real-world scenarios to understand how our brain navigates, perceives, and feels within these environments.

The Gut-Mind Connection: There's a saying, "Trust your gut." As it turns out, our gut might indeed have a say in how we think. Emerging research is revealing a deep connection between our digestive system and our brain, reshaping our understanding of emotions, decisions, and overall well-being.

Nature's Influence on Cognition: Ever felt a burst of clarity after a walk in the woods? Research now delves into how nature – its sights, sounds, and even smells – can influence cognitive processes, from enhancing creativity to reducing stress.

Forecasting the Future: Where Are We Heading?

Brain-Computer Hybrids: The lines between our minds and machines might soon blur. Imagine thinking of a message and having it typed out, without ever touching a keyboard. The fusion of cognitive psychology with technology might soon make this a reality.

The Space Within: As space exploration accelerates, understanding cognition in outer space environments will become crucial. How does zero gravity influence thought? Or how does the vastness of space impact our emotional well-being? These are questions future cognitive psychologists might grapple with.

Universal Cognition: Beyond our species, researchers are increasingly curious about the cognitive processes of other creatures. How do dolphins think? Or what goes on in the mind of an octopus? The answers might reshape our understanding of cognition itself.

As we stand at the cusp of tomorrow, the mysteries of the mind remain as intriguing as ever. Each discovery is a step, not towards an end, but towards newer questions, challenges, and wonders. As the echoes of the future grow louder, we invite you to stay curious, to question, and to explore.

Because, dear reader, every mind is a universe, and there's always more to discover. To infinity and beyond!

Epilogue: The Mind Unleashed – The Odyssey Within and Beyond

As we reach the final pages of our expedition into the marvel that is the human mind, let's take a pause, a deep breath, and reflect on the journey we've undertaken together.

The Invisible Threads: Cognitive Psychology in Your Daily Life

Morning Musing: Every morning, when you decide to hit the snooze button or leap out of bed, cognitive processes are at play. Your memories of past decisions, your understanding of time, and even your emotions all intertwine to influence that seemingly simple choice.

Digital Decisions: Swiping on a dating app? Deciding which photo to post on social media? Your cognitive filters – crafted by past experiences, societal influences, and inherent preferences – are at work, subtly guiding every click and swipe.

Conversations & Connections: Ever found the right words to console a friend or shared a joke that made someone's day? That's the dance of cognition and language, of emotion and empathy, playing out in real time.

The Boundless Odyssey Ahead: Why the Adventure Must Continue

Ever-Changing Enigmas: Just as the cosmos never ceases to evolve, neither does our understanding of the mind. With every passing day, fresh mysteries emerge, beckoning those with insatiable curiosity.

Applied Adventures: From building more intuitive technologies to creating therapeutic practices, the applications of cognitive psychology ripple through every aspect of society. By diving deeper into this field, you could shape a future where technology, therapy, and daily tasks become more human-centric.

The Personal Quest: The journey into cognitive psychology isn't just academic; it's deeply personal. The more you understand about cognition, the more you unearth about yourself – your motivations, fears, desires, and dreams.

In Conclusion...

The pages of this book might have reached their end, but your voyage into the realm of cognitive psychology has only just begun. Let the knowledge you've gained be your compass, guiding you through life's myriad mazes. Let curiosity be your North Star, always leading you towards new horizons.

For in understanding the mind, you not only grasp the essence of humanity but also unlock the infinite potential that resides within you.

Until our paths cross again, dear reader, journey on. For every ending is but a new beginning.

About Freudian Trips

Welcome to Freudian Trips, your dedicated platform for diving deep into the world of psychology. We are more than just a YouTube channel or a book publisher. We are a beacon of enlightenment, making complex psychological concepts accessible and engaging for all.

Our YouTube channel is a rich repository of psychology made simple. We take the profound and often complex ideas from the world of psychology and break them down into digestible, easy-to-understand content. From the foundational theories of Freud to the cognitive insights of Piaget, we cover a broad spectrum of psychological schools and thoughts, making psychology accessible to everyone, regardless of their background or prior knowledge.

As a book publisher, we take the same approach, transforming intricate psychological theories into comprehensible narratives. Our books are not just collections of words, but vessels of wisdom that make psychology approachable and relatable. We believe that psychology should not be confined to academic circles, but should be available to all who seek to understand the human mind and behavior.

At Freudian Trips, we believe in the power of curiosity and the pursuit of knowledge. We are here to stoke the fires of your curiosity, to guide you on your intellectual journey, and to help you navigate the fascinating world of psychology.

If you are someone who is not afraid to question, to explore, and to learn, then you are in the right place. Join us on this journey of exploration, as we make psychology easy to understand, one concept at a time.

Be sure to visit our Youtube channel at: www.freudiantrips.com/youtube

You can also visit us on the web at www.freudiantrips.com

Welcome to The Freudian Trip community. Stay curious. Stay enlightened.

www.ingramcontent.com/pod-product-compliance
Lightning Source LLC
Chambersburg PA
CBHW071016260726
48661CB00007B/2989